HOW DID THE ANCIENT AFRICAN EMPIRES GET THEIR GOODS?

HISTORY BOOKS GRADE 3

Children's History Books

BABY PROFESSOR
EDUCATION KIDS

Speedy Publishing LLC

40 E. Main St. #1156

Newark, DE 19711

www.speedypublishing.com

Copyright 2017

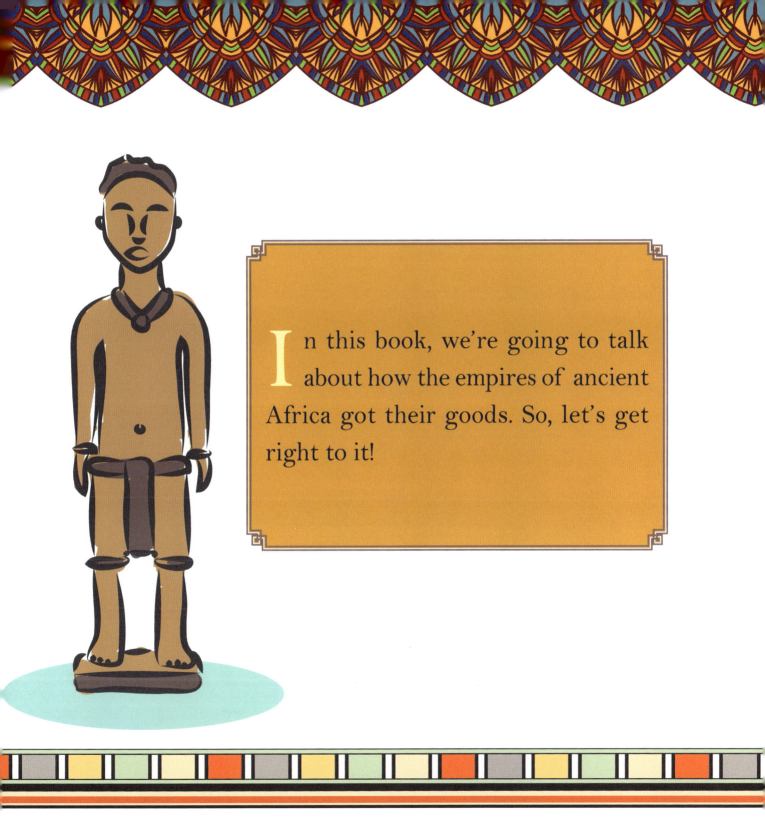

In this book, we're going to talk about how the empires of ancient Africa got their goods. So, let's get right to it!

Trade has always been a very important part of the African economy as far back as ancient times. Africans have been selling to traders from West Asia and India and buying goods from them since about 4000 Bc.

African traders also traded among the different empires in Africa. For money, they used cowrie shells, as did civilizations in China and India.

WHAT DID AFRICAN TRADERS BUY AND SELL?

◇◇◇◇◇◇◇◇◇◇◇◇◇

One of the first exports from Africa was ivory, which came from elephant tusks. The Egyptians and the populations in West Asia used ivory to make elaborate jewelry as well as fine furniture.

SELLING IVORY

OSTRICH EGGS

The African traders also sold enormous ostrich eggs and wood that came from their forests.

GOLD

Hard stones, in the forms of diorite as well as granite, were popular trade items as well. One of their most important exports was gold.

ANCIENT BEEDS FROM
ETHIOPIA

The traders from Kush purchased many types of items from Egypt, West Asia, and from the Phoenician civilization, which was known for its glass making. They bought cloth, such as linen and cotton. They also bought glass beads, other glass items, perfumes, and wines.

By the year 500 BC, traders in the north part of Africa as well as Egypt were using coins for money instead of cowrie shells. The coins were made with gold and silver and sometimes with bronze. These types of coins were invented by West Africans. Ships transported traders from West Asia and India to the eastern coast of Africa to trade.

ZANZIBAR PYSA COIN

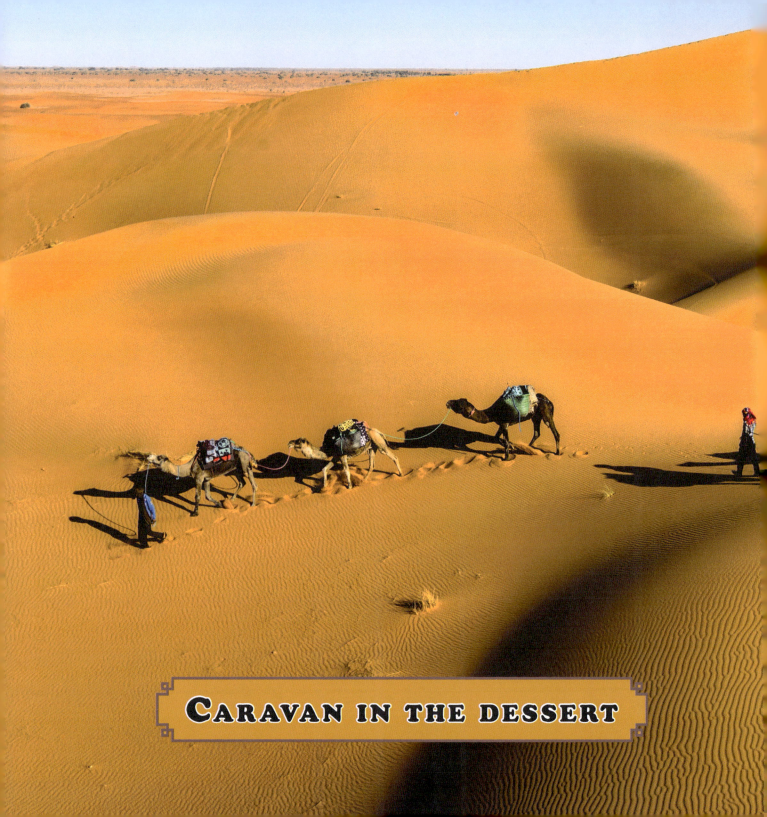

CARAVAN IN THE DESSERT

round 500 AD, a new invention changed the way goods were being transported. An improved saddle for the camel had been invented. Long caravans with an average of 1,000 camels began to cross the hot Sahara Desert in order to trade goods with the populations of West Africa.

The traders brought salt with them from locations south of the desert. They traded the salt with the kingdom of Ghana in exchange for the gold from the West African mines.

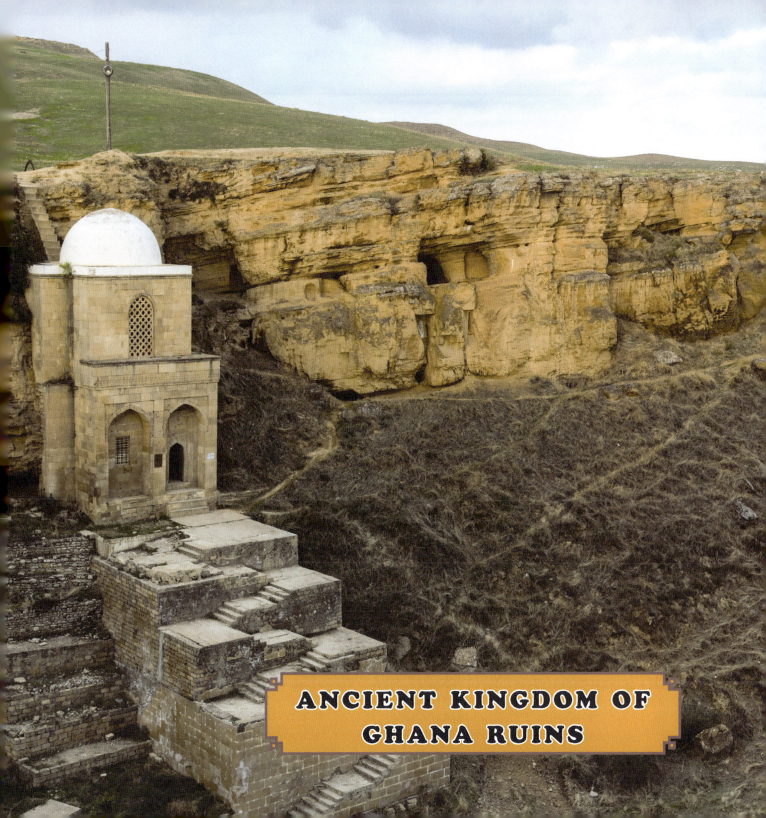

ANCIENT KINGDOM OF
GHANA RUINS

Africans living in the southern kingdoms were trading with the countries of West Asia and India as well. They traded ostrich eggs to get glass beads from India.

Indian glass beads that had been transported from East Africa have been found in Zimbabwe as well as the Congo. The African traders also sold ivory and precious metals including copper and gold.

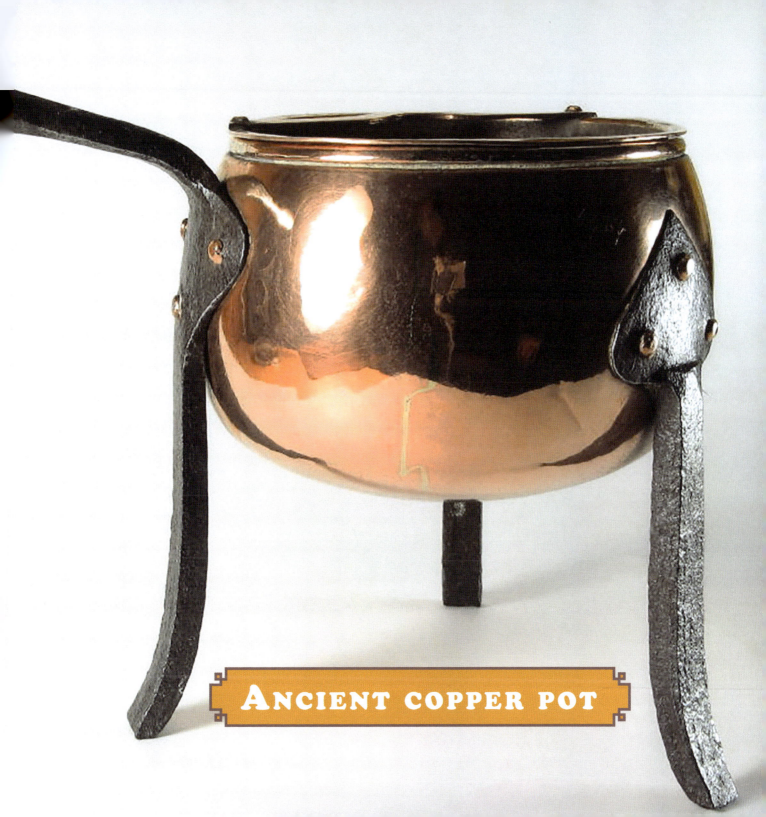

Ancient copper pot

In 600 AD, the slave trade began, and the African traders sold men as well as women into a life of enslavement to Egyptian masters. With the money they received from the slaves they purchased wheat, wine, different types of cloth, and sugar. The Byzantine Empire purchased ivory from the African traders and in exchange offered jewelry and objects made of glass.

SLAVE TRADE

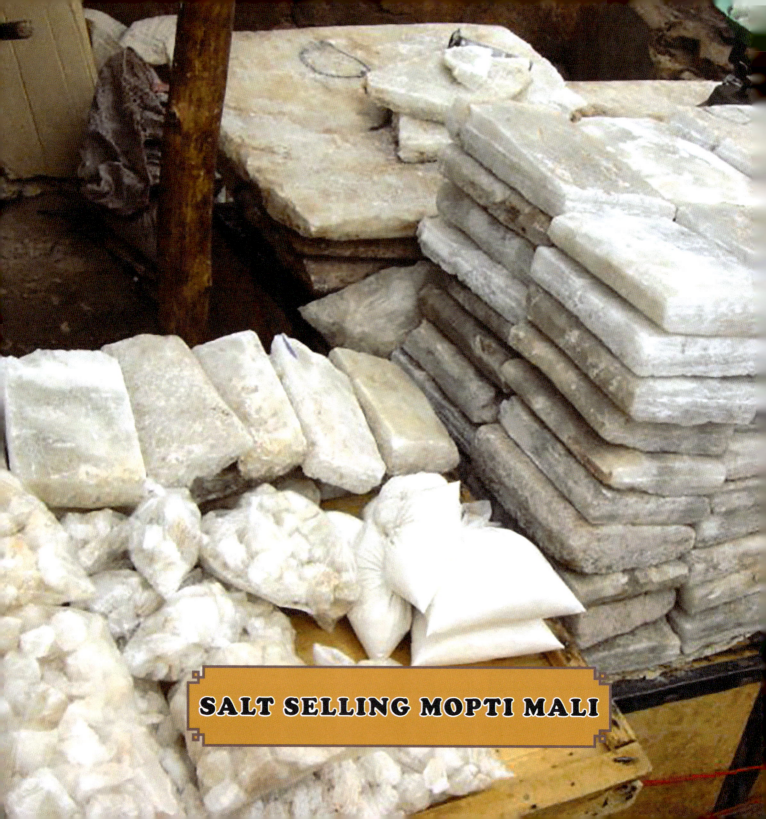

SALT SELLING MOPTI MALI

THE SALT-GOLD TRADE

◇◇◇◇◇◇◇◇◇◇◇◇◇◇◇◇◇◇

The empire of Ghana became very prosperous based on the trading of salt and gold that took place between the empires in Western Africa and those in Northern Africa. This trade exchange was very critical, and, as a result, the kingdom of Ghana controlled gold as well as salt and all the trade routes that journeyed through the kingdom.

WHY WAS THE SALT-GOLD TRADE IMPORTANT?

◇◇◇◇◇◇◇◇◇◇◇◇◇◇◇◇◇◇

The population of North Africa wanted to purchase gold and the people in West Africa desperately needed salt. South of Ghana, in a place named Wangara, the desert sun was intensely hot.

GOLD BARS

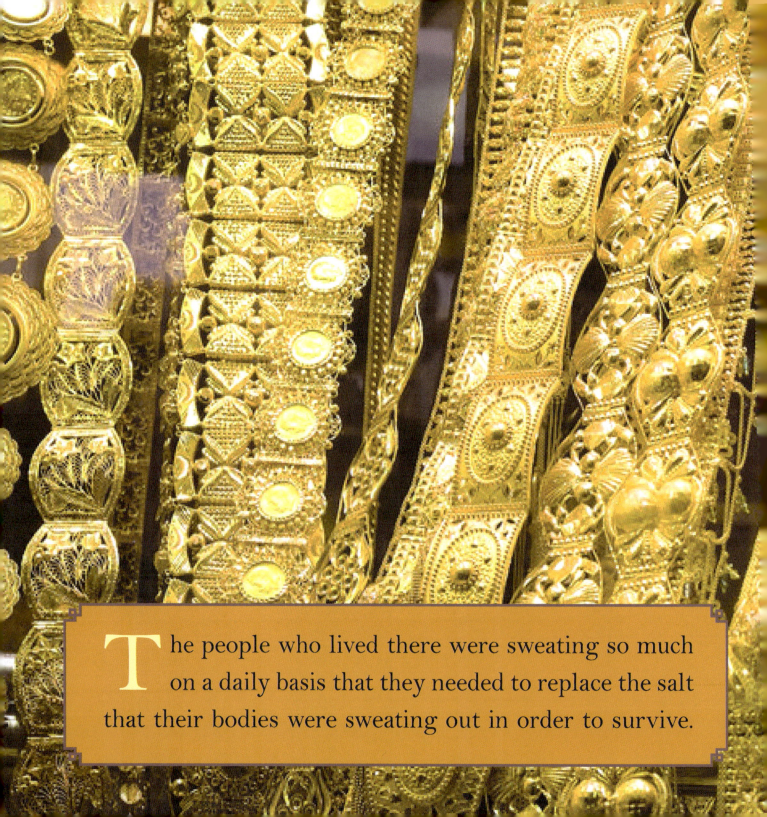

The people who lived there were sweating so much on a daily basis that they needed to replace the salt that their bodies were sweating out in order to survive.

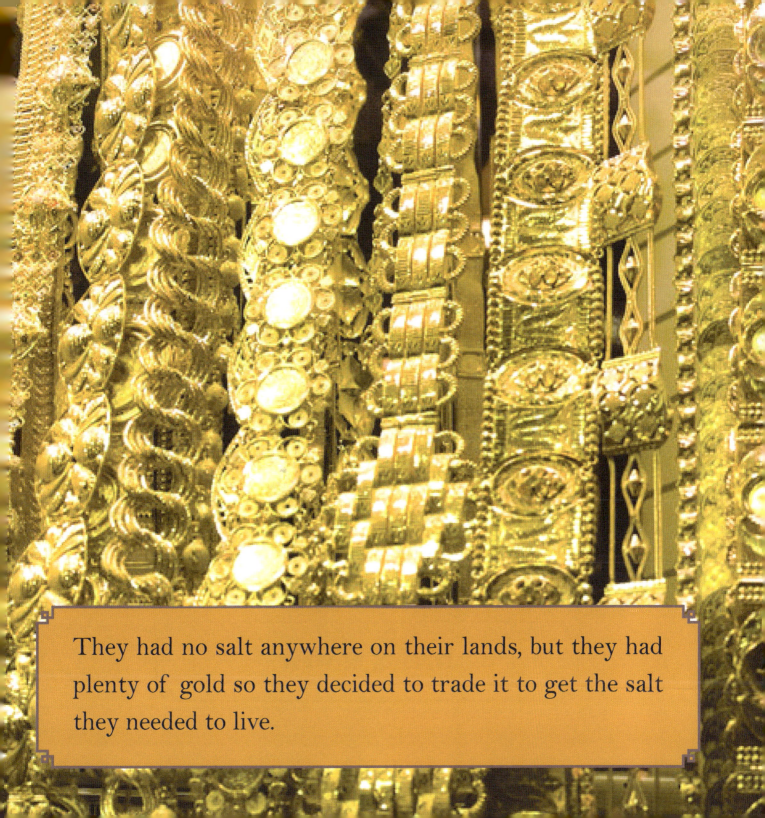

They had no salt anywhere on their lands, but they had plenty of gold so they decided to trade it to get the salt they needed to live.

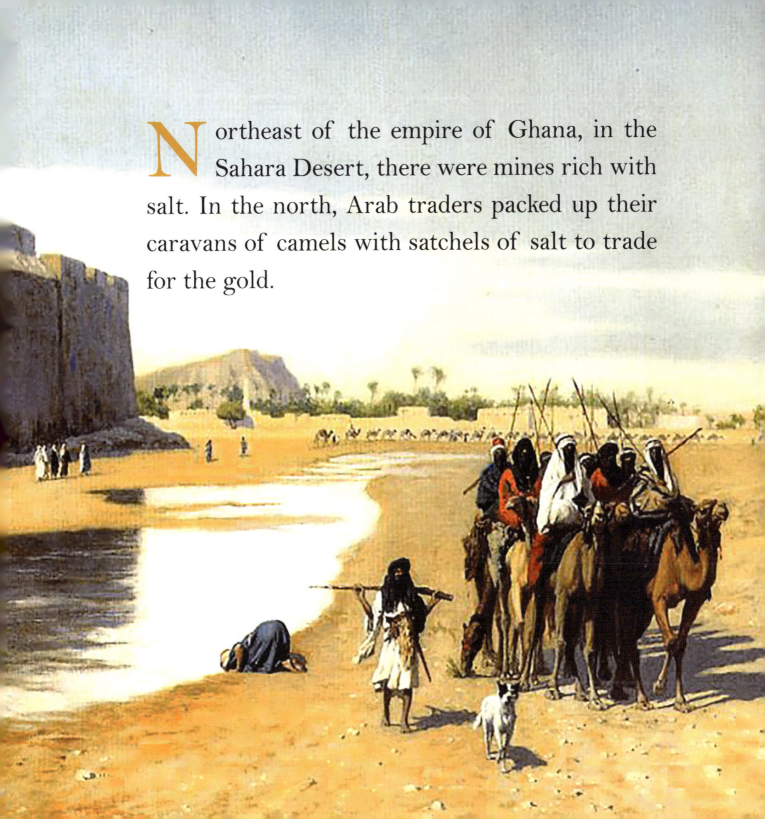

Northeast of the empire of Ghana, in the Sahara Desert, there were mines rich with salt. In the north, Arab traders packed up their caravans of camels with satchels of salt to trade for the gold.

All the traders had to pass through the empire of Ghana so the empire became a "middleman" in the transaction. Salt wasn't the only type of item brought from the north. Dried fruit as well as cotton cloth, pieces of leather, and copper items were brought for the trade as well.

LEATHER

ANCIENT GHANA

THE SILENT BARTER

◇◇◇◇◇◇◇◇◇◇◇◇◇◇◇◇◇◇

When the traders from the north arrived in Ghana, the process for trading was done in secret. The traders who had salt and those who had gold never saw each other! The reason was that the location of the gold mines was secret. The trading was set up in a process that the traders agreed to follow called silent barter.

The traders from the north stacked up their salt along the banks of a river so the gold traders from Wangara could inspect what they had brought. Drumbeats announced that the goods were ready for inspection and at that point the northern traders left and traveled several miles away.

Then, the Wangara gold traders came to the location and inspected the salt piles carefully. They placed bags of gold dust next to the piles they wanted to buy and promptly left.

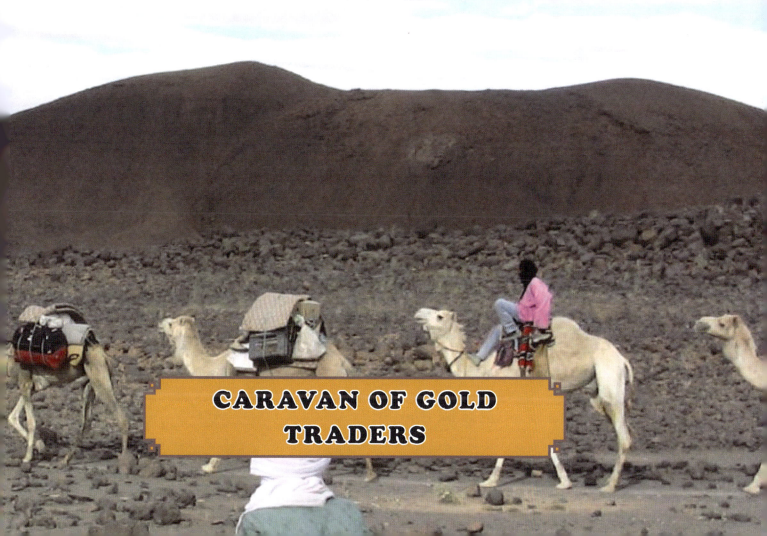

CARAVAN OF GOLD TRADERS

SALT

At a later time, the traders from the north came back. If they were happy with the gold dust that had been offered in exchange, they took it. If not, the process continued in the same manner until each side was pleased with the result. It was believed that the salt and the gold were equivalent in value. The traders from each side traded the goods without ever seeing each other face to face.

The king of Ghana became incredibly wealthy since he only allowed the traders to use gold dust for their trade. The larger nuggets ended up belonging to him and to the empire. The king also built up the kingdom's wealth by charging taxes to the traders who used the routes in Ghana.

TEMPLE OF APEDAMAK RUINS

Rawak

The traders were each charged one gold coin, which was a dinar, when they entered the empire and two when they left. The traders didn't resent this tariff, because the money was partially used to keep them safe. Ghana was known as a place where trading could take place safely.

The salt-gold trade was thriving in the empire until around 1250 AD. At that point, the Muslims attacked the empire and tried to convert the populations to Islam. In addition to that goal, it was their goal to gain control over the salt-gold trade because they knew it would bring them wealth. The empire of Ghana fought the Muslims for over thirty years, but eventually the violence caused the empire to collapse.

LARABANGA MOSQUE GHANA

TIMBUKTU

MAJOR TRADE CITIES AND ROUTES

◇◇◇◇◇◇◇◇◇◇◇

As the trade routes became established across Africa, major cities grew in population since they were trade centers. In the western section of the continent, Timbuktu and Sijilmasa were two important trade cities as were Gao and Agadez.

S eaports also became important, as goods were brought back and forth by ship. Along the northern coast, Marrakesh and Cairo were important seaports. The city of Adulis located on the Red Sea also became a critical trading hub.

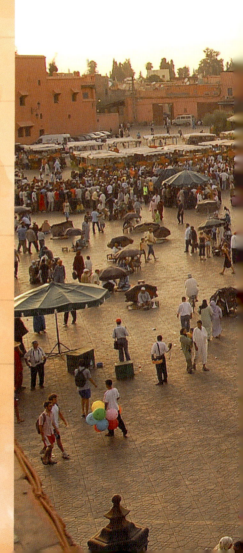

MARAKESH TODAY

Caravans transported goods across the Sahara Desert. They began in Western or Central Africa, traveled across, and then arrived at the trade centers that were close to the coastline and the Mediterranean Sea.

One of the important routes took traders from Timbuktu across the desert to Sijilmasa, which was just south of the port of Marrakesh. Other standard routes were the ones from the city of Gao to the port of Tunis and from the port of Cairo to the city of Agadez in Central Africa.

LONG CARAVANS CROSS THE SAHARA

The large groups of people and animals that traveled across the desert sands were caravans. Camels were the major type of transportation and they were put into service carrying goods and supplies as well as people. Slaves sometimes hauled goods also.

CARAVAN OF TRADERS

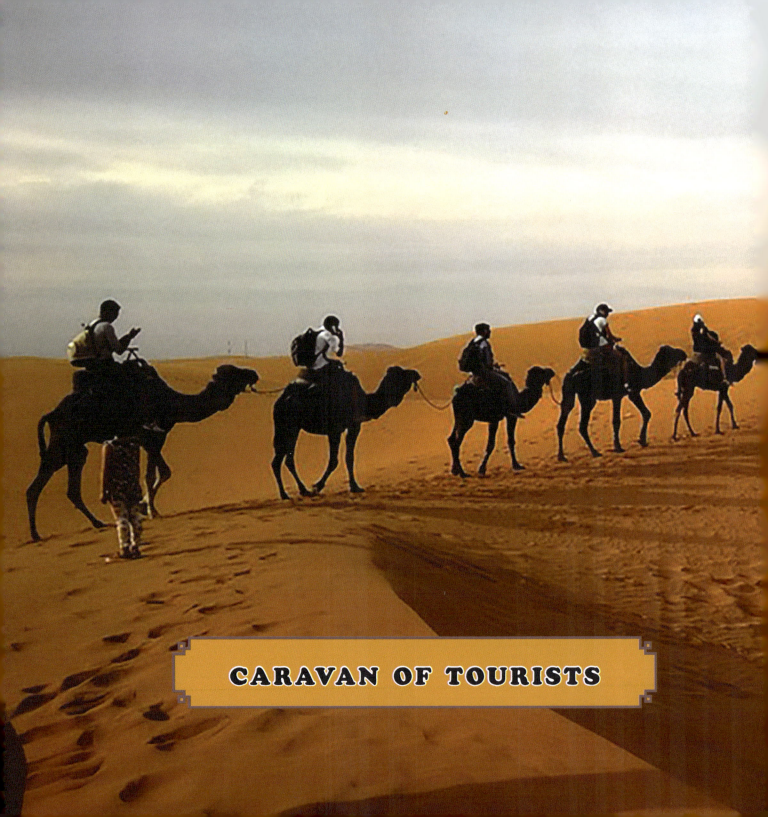

CARAVAN OF TOURISTS

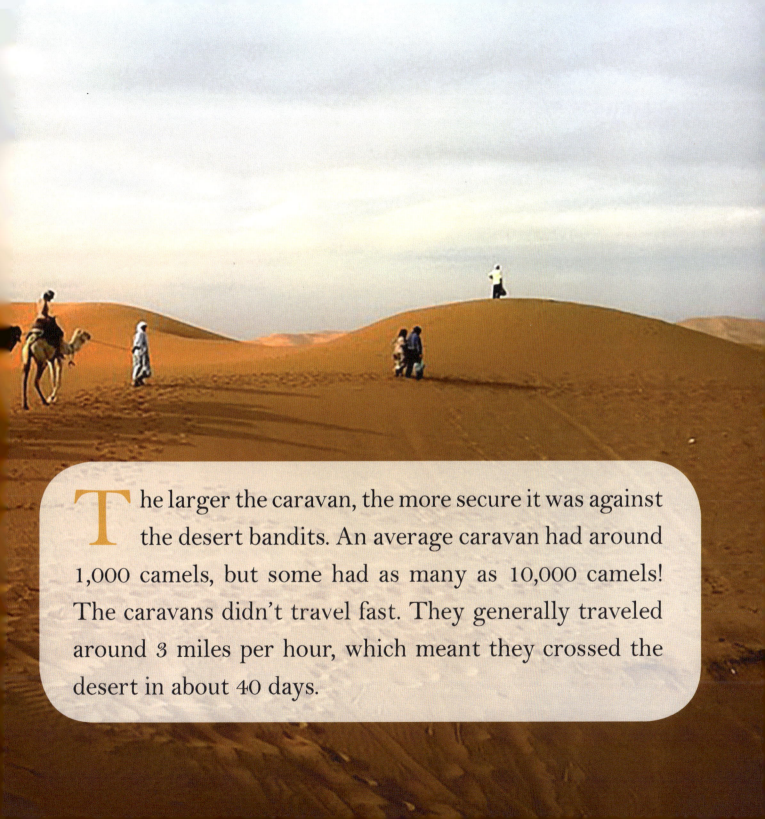

The larger the caravan, the more secure it was against the desert bandits. An average caravan had around 1,000 camels, but some had as many as 10,000 camels! The caravans didn't travel fast. They generally traveled around 3 miles per hour, which meant they crossed the desert in about 40 days.

THE DESERT CAMELS

◇◇◇◇◇◇◇◇◇◇◇◇◇◇◇◇◇◇◇◇

Without the desert camels, a trade route across the mighty Sahara desert wouldn't have been possible. The Berbers, a group of people in the northern part of Africa, domesticated camels about 300 AD. Camels had adapted to living in the desert and could stay alive for very long periods of time with little to no water.

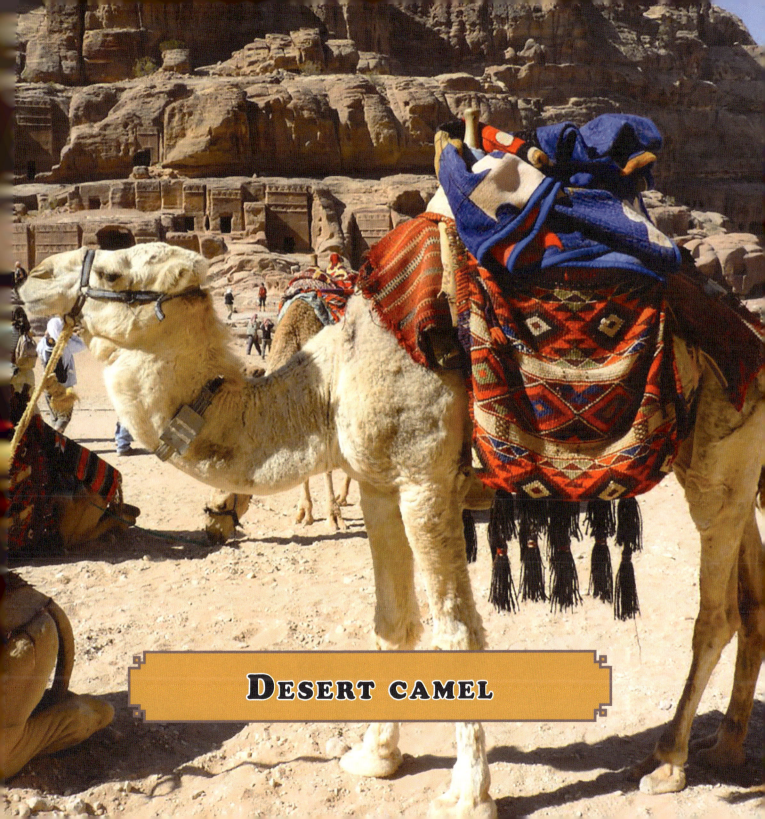

DESERT CAMEL

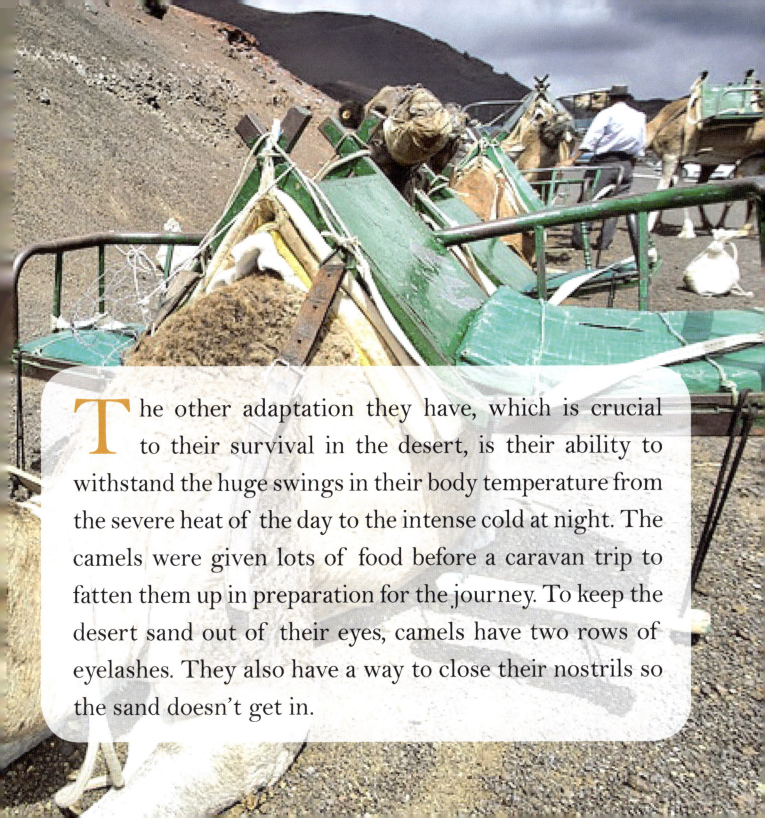

The other adaptation they have, which is crucial to their survival in the desert, is their ability to withstand the huge swings in their body temperature from the severe heat of the day to the intense cold at night. The camels were given lots of food before a caravan trip to fatten them up in preparation for the journey. To keep the desert sand out of their eyes, camels have two rows of eyelashes. They also have a way to close their nostrils so the sand doesn't get in.

Awesome! Now you know more about what types of goods were traded and how goods were transported to ancient Africa. You can find more History books from Baby Professor by searching the website of your favorite book retailer.

Visit

BABY PROFESSOR
EDUCATION KIDS

www.BabyProfessorBooks.com

to download Free Baby Professor eBooks
and view our catalog of new and exciting
Children's Books

Printed in Great Britain
by Amazon